Grand Rising copyright © 2025 by Kiana Nicole

All rights reserved.

Printed in The United States of America

ISBN:

978-1-7343514-2-2

Grand Rising

Also by Kiana Nicole

Ecstasy & Her Blues

This is the key to self mastery

Contents:

You Are The Key

The Unprofessional

Dancing In The Reign

Love Is King

The Elephant In The Room Is You

Me, You & Our Sun

The Grand Finale: Sunset

Grand Rising

There is a moment in every life when the dawn feels different.

The light touches your skin not just as warmth but as a call.

An invitation to rise. Not just from sleep, but from the past,

from fear, from everything that has kept you small.

This book is a journey through that rising.

It is for the ones who have felt the weight of yesterday

but refuse to let it define today.

It is a reminder that no matter how dark the night,

the sun will rise again.

Grand rising is more than a greeting— it is a state of being.

You are being awakened, enlightened, and remembered.

This is your rising.

You Are The Key

God is thee creative director.

Leadership

Your rising is community service
because when you rise, you lead.
As a good leader, you encourage others to do the same.
You encourage others to find their key.
Not all will follow, not all will see,
but a true leader plants the seed.

You Are The Key

Too often we resist change,
we resist letting go, we resist a new paradigm,
we resist a new story.
We run from ourselves. Running on autopilot.
Oblivious to the ways in which we self sabotage
because staying in a low vibrational frequency is easy.
It's comfortable and familiar.
We don't go far like this.
Instead, you trap yourself in your own mind
when the entire time,

You are the key.

We have what it takes to move on and tell a new story.
Be the key that gives yourself a chance to unlock more life.
Don't dim your light.
Use it to be a pioneer,
an alchemist,
a trailblazer,
a star.

Lock In

"The world is yours"-- but at what cost?
What did you build and what was lost?
Did you trade your voice for another throne?
Did you drift too far from your inner home?

Lock into what you've always known.
Even though you may wander, wild and far.
Your heart remembers exactly who you are.

Dedicate all of you to the vision you are creating.
Not chasing love, not seeking light.
But being it – so divine.
This is your birthright.

You have to be the thing that saves you
or else you lock yourself out of your own dream.

You unlock the world by locking in.

*Old keys can't unlock new doors.
Our next life will cost us this one.*

North Star

Dare to dream beyond what's safe.
You'll rise, you'll grow, you'll expand.
You'll land in a higher place than you imagined…

When the road is unclear and you can't see the way ahead,
trust that stars align when you're being led
by the most high, north star;
knows your prayers before you speak.
Even in darkness, it guides the brave and the weak.
Let it guide you to do the shadow work.
Which then ultimately leads you to
who you're meant to be all along.
Your purpose is rooted in who and what you needed for yourself.

What makes you shine?

It's already written in the stars…
It's yours.
It always has been and always will be.
All you have to do is aim for the stars and shoot for the moon.

The Blueprint

I had to rise to the occasion.

I knew I was great but I had to add some persuasion.

See me on a Sunday and I'll never look like

the dark times I was facing.

Let's face it, heavy is the head that wears the crown.

I had to doggy paddle and keep my chin up so that I won't drown.

I had to swim across the ocean and the waters so blue

they think it's cool when I tell my story.

But let me tell you how hard it's been to reach my glory...

It's been breathtaking,

backbreaking,

heart aching,

plenty of decision makings...

Who would've thought that the route I chose would be scenic.

I had to shoot my shot just to look back at the hoops

I jumped through;

just to learn how to move wise.

Missed a few times, but I still kept a true eye.

Now I don't flinch when the fear tries to cruise by.

Bars too hard it goes over their heads.

That's why the best sits at the top of the shelf.

Yeah, I'm hard to reach.

I'll be sitting at the top of the mountain

they thought I couldn't move.

Crazy part is, I haven't even peaked.

What's good is subjective, to each their own.

All I know is this is mine and mine alone.

It's all divinely orchestrated.

They tried to dismiss me like I'm uneducated
because my moves couldn't be calculated.
I guess they found me to be intimidating
because I couldn't be manipulated.
So articulate, I completely annihilated.

That's what happens when you stay in a lane of your own
and never lack persistence or dedication.
Why would I wait for your validation,
when my seat at the table has been designated?
I've been graduated.
I used to write blues, now I write the blueprint.
Even if you took notes, you could never model.
I'm a hard act to follow…

Trailblazer

From land to land

my heart is too big for comfort.

I've always been a land rover,

my range is immeasurable.

My words are impeccable.

Rage in these words and so is my calm.

This is my inner monologue.

It's always been me versus me so this is my own dialogue.

I'm just blazing the trail I'm embarking

if that means building my catalog.

Pen is a tool and voice is a bridge.

I'm trying to bring heaven on earth.

Let's make a way to bring what's inside of us,

to what's in front of us.

I know it probably seems so distant

but we're closer than you think.

I'm the one trying to build unity

instead of being stuck on an island with no community.

This is my commute.

From land to land, overseas;

connecting the dots spiritually.

Who talks about the people who had to build bridges like these?

They never care about the mission,

only care about the story when it unfolds.

But who listens for what goes untold?

Natural Disaster

Do you think the world is ending?

No, but the world as we know it is.

*Always prepare for a plot twist
by practicing the art of detachment.*

Victoria

I'm still that girl on the run like I used to be on the track team.

I was too big stepping for them to run against me.

Should've called me the coach the way I ran the whole team.

They followed my footsteps trying to be just like me.

But I'll tell you one thing; they could never replicate this.

They could never tell my story like

they know what it is to walk in my shoes.

I'm too much of a player,

you could never keep track of my moves.

I went and embarked on different avenues.

Like a jack of all trades;

Riddle me this, riddle me that.

Little me is impressed with where I'm at.

I've always been a wild cat.

I see the signs reminding me that I'm right on track.

In the field, I got people counting me out

but God has my back.

Pushing me to victory.

You are the center of a circle you can't see.

Spring Cleaning

Practicing the art of detachment.

I've cut all the dead ends,

I've taken the road less traveled,

I've distanced myself from everyone.

I've been finding my own way to go about things.

I've been sitting with everything.

Getting to the root of it all.

Letting go of a lot. I can't hold too much in,

I can't keep too much on me,

I can't get too comfortable.

I've been purging,

I've been detoxing,

I've been decluttering.

In every way, shape and form;

I let it all go.

I made space.

The air is cleared.

I feel lighter now.

Spring always makes you spiral first before you bounce back.

Legacy

Let me share my words with you
just to affirm my love language.
I'll lay it all on the line.
I'll tell you I love you;
I'll scream it from the mountain tops.
I hope the echoes hold you long after I'm gone
just to remind you I'm still here.

Even when my words fall short,
I hope you understand my silence.
I hope you understand when I go ghost.
I hope you still feel my presence.
I hope you know my spirit is free.
I hope you don't hold on to hope too tight,
so tight that you forget to let me go.
Hoping I would stay a while…
I told you I wasn't to be held for too long.

Let me be free
and may you find peace.

Can you see it through?

Can you see how I show up in many ways?

I hope you count this one.

This one is the way I know best.

I've been trying to reach you for some time now.

You always seem so busy with work

or caught in your travel plans.

I love that for you.

When will you take a moment to acknowledge my words?

You're a free spirit, I get that.

Wait til life lets you be freer than the body you call home.

So busy with work, did you do the inside job?

You might have traveled far, but have you traveled deep?

Sit with that for a moment.

Do you know your legacy?

How else would you rise above?

Legacy looks different for everybody.
Just like I love that for you,
can you love this for me?
I left this here for you.
Did you get my message?
I'll say it loud and clear;
I'll say it soft spoken and half broken;
I say all this to say,
yeah, I said it.

I said it cause I heard your cries before I saw your tears drop.
So I wrote this so I can cry with you.
I wrote this to remind you I've been there too.
Ancestors coming through;
They said it's bigger than you.
I hope you see it through.
I hope you see how I show up in many ways.
I hope you count this one.
I said it the best I could.
May you find peace in my pieces.
Perfectly imperfect.
Just know I gave it my all,
down to my last breath…

Staying Alive

They love to see my pain.

They love to see me left in the rain.

They love to say my name in vain.

They love when I'm going insane.

They love when I ain't popping champagne

or doing my damn thing.

But I'll do it one more time just to show you I'll do it again.

They hate you, then they love you, then they hate you again.

They love when I'm not too over the top.

They love to see my tears drop.

They wanna see my heart stop.

But I'm more alive than ever.

They hate to see how I alchemize pain.

They hate to see the rain turn into my reign.

They hate to say my name cause this ain't no plain jane.

They hate that they can't snatch my chain.

They hate to admit I'm good at this game.

The Alchemist

Have you ever lost your identity

and existed solely as your entity?

Have you ever sat with your pain?

Have you ever called your demons by name?

Have you ever looked your shadow in the face?

At some point in life you're forced to dive that deep within yourself.

Alchemy teaches us how to transmute energy.

Discipline and obedience,

stillness and silence.

When you listen closely,

life speaks to you in miraculous ways.

I learned how to transform pain into power.

I created something out of nothing.

I made sure everything I touched turned into gold.

I became attractive without chasing.

I became attractive by being my most authentic self.

I became attractive because I have a special kind of spirit.

The kind of spirit you meet when you're on the path of

enlightenment.

I studied for hours,

I ran for miles,

I slept on the floor,

I cried for weeks,

I sobered up,

I fought a good fight,

Then I surrendered to the life God had for me.

Reflection of You

I'm here to challenge your limiting beliefs.

I'm here to call you out.

I'm here to trigger you.

I'm here to remind you of your patience.

I'm here to show you what strength looks like

in the face of adversity.

How else would we recognize ourselves without a mirror?

Discovering your inner flame,

let's you recognize your twin flame.

Love, Knaura

Dear you,

This is where photography meets poetry.

Where romance meets novelty.

Where life meets memory.

What an honor it is to be a part of the gallery.

A collection,

a memorial,

a gift.

You are the apple of my eye.

There is something so special

and intimate about documenting life.

Real, raw emotions.

Glimpses of expression.

Art is everywhere.

Beauty is in the eye of the beholder.

My hands hold history.

Crafting masterpieces,

shaping the invisible,

giving form to spirit.

Making the sacred become seen

because I am a witness of the divine.

A lover of stories that transcend time.

Remembering what's lost,

collecting what's been found.

A creator creating different faces over and over…

until you recognize God.

Love, Knaura

The Unprofessional

Draft Day

You can feel when you're being called

into the next chapter of your life.

The draft is rough but you were chosen

for this position for a reason.

Step into another part of who you are.

Allow yourself to start all over again.

Allow yourself to be taught a new lesson.

Allow yourself to be shown a different light.

Allow yourself to pivot into who you're being called to be.

Dress up and make it real.

Look like you came to win.

Walk in the room like God sent you.

Study your assignment so you can show up as your best.

Even if you're being called to be a part

of yourself you haven't fully discovered yet.

You can find out the details later…

If you want to change your life,

you have to change your approach.

You have to change your narrative.

You have to change your entire state of mind.

Only then will you change the trajectory of your life.

Ego

Let me clean my act up...
It's easy to be myself behind four walls
but once I stepped outside,
I felt like I needed to dress up.
It was very performative of me.
I didn't know how to rest in my being.
I just wanted to be the girl you thought highly of
so I put myself on a pedestal.
I had to live up to her.
I loved her but she was killing me.
I was afraid if you really knew me...
you wouldn't love me the same.
I wanted you to love me to keep me sane.
Honestly, it's driving me insane.
It's become embarrassing to say the least.
But my ego needed to be stripped.
The vulnerability gave me strength.
The humility made me more human.

I had to put my pride aside,

I had to stop people pleasing,

I had to show up for me,

I had to sit down with myself and remember who I am.

I stopped living up to your expectations of me.

I stopped trying to fit into your standards.

I stopped playing in your narrative.

I wanted the shoe to fit.

Truth is, one size doesn't fit all

so let me stop playing small.

Let me clean my act up…

I started living in my own truth.

Now I value a minimalistic lifestyle.

I never had to do too much to be loved.

I let my hair down,

I smudged my red lips,

I used to paint my nails red, now I keep it clear.

Is it clear that I've become comfortable in my own skin?

I like it better when I don't have to play pretend.

I like it better when you like me for who I am.

Who I am can be respected more.

Who I am can be loved more;

because who I am can finally be seen.

*I am blind when I live life on my own terms.
It's only when I follow God's lead,
that my vision becomes clear.*

Therapy

I'm trying not to crash out.

I'm trying not to self sabotage.

I'm trying not to repeat my old ways.

This is my new vice.

It's all new but it's something I knew

I would have to come back to

so I can understand my patterns of destruction.

So I can build my happy place.

Even when it's not the happiest;

at least I know how to navigate.

Let me tell you about why it's hard for me to open up.

About why I could never settle for too long

and why I'm constantly in a state of fight or flight.

Therapy is a soft room with sharp edges.

It slices me open and asks me to feel…

She asked, where does it hurt the most?
I sat in silence trying to detect where it hurts…

Some pain has no location.
It lives in the pause between words,
in the nights I spend alone;
in the mirror I can't face.
If I put my pain anywhere, I bury it beneath my bones.
It feels like I carry the world on my back.
My feet hold all the weight
and I have bruises that don't show…

She listened.
She didn't rush me.
She waited for me to continue
as if silence had value.
As if I had value here.

I was always the strong one, I admitted.
The one who knew how to soothe
and smile even when it aches.

Tears came without warning…

She handed me tissues like grief had a seat at the table.

I whispered… *I'm so tired of being strong.*

She said, t*hen let's learn softness.*

Silence always felt safer to me.

You survived by disappearing, she said.

But healing will ask you to come back

to sit with silence until she finds her voice.

I don't know who I am without pain, I said.

I told her how I push people away to see if they'll come back;

just to see if I'm real to them.

Sometimes I don't know
who I am unless someone is loving me or leaving me.

That sounds exhausting, she said.

It is, and lonely.
I ruin things, I said.
Even when I don't want to.
I just want to feel safe inside myself.

What do you know for sure about yourself? She asked.

I feel like a different person in every room I enter.
Will it always be this hard to trust my own feelings?
I feel like I'm too much…

For who, she asked?
For the people I love.

What if they were never meant to
be the ones who could hold you? she said.

You're not too much,
you're just used to people who only love pieces of you.
But real love loves you in its entirety.
The storm and the stillness.

I closed my eyes for a moment...
Imagining someone seeing all of me
without flinching.
I imagined me without performing
or apologizing.

Finally I said, *sometimes peace feels foreign.*

You're learning safety in a nervous system that only knows survival, she said.

Another Day

Another day I have to get out of bed.

I can't lay here and dwell for too long.

So I sit up at the edge

trying to find the strength

to face a world that wants me to play along.

So I dress up for the day.

Like I haven't been sad all night.

But I can't look like what I've been through.

So I have to make my face up.

I took a long time getting ready to exist

but I am here and I am thankful for another day.

Survival of the Fittest

Most people will literally lose their minds
trying to be a part of a reality that isn't real.
But business is business.
Are you minding yours?
People do a lot of things just to fit in.
You're supposed to be outstanding.
Standing firm in what you believe in.

They don't want us to think for ourselves.
They want population,
they want control,
they want power,
they want our souls.

Too many people mindlessly play only for the score.
you win the game when you know what you're playing for.
Live in your God given purpose.

Be a creator of your environment rather than a product of it.

What I love about God is that he shows up even when we're crashing out to remind us to stay in our lane.

The Art of Intelligence

Knowledge is like having a library of books.

Discernment is knowing which books to read and apply.

Wisdom is our ability to understand what we know.

Intelligence takes all three and influences our ability to

learn, adapt and continuously grow.

Intelligence is revolutionary.

I have mastered turning my insanity into creativity and this is where I thrive.

Abundance

I needed a new perspective on life.

I needed clarity.

I needed a break through that'll help me see things clearly.

I had a tower moment.

Everything I had built up came crashing down.

I've been humiliated,

I've been devastated,

I've been broken in ways I couldn't imagine coming back from.

The frame of my mind has been completely destroyed.

You would think a tornado flew around my room;

all to make room for bigger blessings.

I had to trust the divine to guide me on a new path

hoping somehow a greater reality was upon me.

I was reminded Rome wasn't built in a day

so as I was moving into a new year

and discovering a new me,

I decided I'll dance my way there.

It's in the moments when I step into grace,

that I step into alignment.

I find my every move to be more balanced, more intentional.

Every twist and turn becomes easier.

Embracing the journey through movement.

Intune with the flow of life.

A reminder that life doesn't have to be perfect to be beautiful.

Just dance in abundance.

Will you be more loyal to the identity you've known than the destiny you're being called to?

First Class

God is the teacher.

We are the students.

Earth is the classroom.

The lesson is in nature.

God is everywhere.

A trickster, a treater.

Both chaos and calm.

Gentle and demanding.

The teacher says…

learn or you won't survive.

The Other Side

On the other side of discomfort is growth.

On the other side of darkness is light.

On the other side of pain is power.

Let me walk you home if we're taking it there…

On the other side of your one bedroom apartment is a nice house.

On the other side of your miscarriage is a newborn.

On the other side of your divorce is a new love.

On the other side of your rod is a big fish.

On the other side of your hard work is the fruits of your labor.

Because on the other side of your misery is a happy place.

Remember sidewalks are parallel to one another.

All you have to do is cross the road.

All you have to do is take the leap.

I promise you will land on your feet.

*Every time you wanna go back,
remember the reason why you left.*

Balance

Life is about balance.
Too much of anything is never a good thing.
Careful not to over indulge.
It's easy to get caught up in a high.
Can't let none of this shit throw me off balance.
Can't let none of this move me.
I got my own motion.
I had to change the narrative.
Can't move out of e-motion.
Can't let none of it take me out of my character.
Can't let none of it knock me off my feet.
My boundaries are solid.
My discernment is the rock.
Standing ten toes; following the yellow brick road.
Goodness comes back to me tenfold.
Doing self care in my white robe.
Walking on a tightrope.
Trying to put the balance in my account now.
I have to take accountability.
I have to admit, it's my fault.

My fault I needed more stability.

Mentally, emotionally, physically, spiritually.

I thought all I needed was flexibility.

Stretching myself too thin trying to balance everything.

Discipline became my priority.

Following my silver lining;

that's gotta count for something!

Poetic Justice

I've said many things…

I've said many things that you didn't like.

I've said many truths too passionately.

My delivery has come off too aggressively;

It backfired on me.

I tasted my own medicine.

My words are too bitter to swallow.

I got a knot in my throat.

I got to let it out.

Speak my mind.

In light of this,

You said many things…

You said many things I didn't like.

You said many truths too passionately.

The message has been delivered to my front door;

knocking loud and clear.

I understand where you're coming from.

I've been there.

We've said many things…

Nobody has to get attacked;

only bring truth to light.

It's not supposed to end in a fight.

I hope you understand where I'm coming from.

Let's not get lost in translation,

I'll translate it for you…

I love you

I love you

I love you

In the most passionate way ever.

Violet

To the woman trying to understand the grand scheme
when life distracts you from yourself;
You can hardly remember your own name.

Lost and found.

All at once…

She started seeing red.
She started turning blue.
She has her emotions confused.
So she sits out on the green grass.
She soaks in the big yellow sun.
She starts to feel all the hues.
She starts to recollect her memory.
She remembers she paints for a living
but purple is nowhere to be found.
A necessary color to complete the big picture.
It frustrates her so she leaves it alone for a while.
She goes to prepare dinner and the phone rings…
The caller leaves a message…

'Hey Violet, just checking up on you. How's the painting going?

I'm so excited to see you

and your work at the art exhibit this weekend.

I know how long you've waited for this.

I'm so proud of you!'

...

An art exhibit?!

My painting will be up for people to see?

It finally makes sense...

I wasn't searching for purple, I was searching for *myself*...

My name is Violet and

my painting is called *'The Grand Scheme"*

The Grand Scheme

I hear sounds of the grand piano playing

as I enter the art exhibit.

The gallery is beautiful.

My friend walks over,

'Hey Violet,' she says

"Could you explain to me what this painting means to you?"

'The grand scheme isn't linear or loud

It's quiet and ethereal.

Like a natural mystic floating through the air...

There is beauty born from contrast.

The way the day bleeds into night fall.

Ever fading, ever vast.

I paint the unseen rhythm

that ties the heavens to the heart.

To remind the world that in the grand scheme –

We are all shades of violet;

becoming art.

The Perfect Woman

I spent my early twenties trying to become her.

I thought she was the most beautiful.

I thought she knew *everything* there is to know about

being the perfect wife,

being the perfect mother,

being the perfect daughter,

being the perfect sister,

being the perfect writer.

I spent years trying to model what it looks like

until I realized I could never be her

because she doesn't exist.

So I stopped trying to model what they told me I should be.

I gave up the idea of this perfect woman

and I granted myself some grace.

I reminded myself I would never be perfect.

Then I promised myself I would be authentic.

The definition of true beauty.

This brought me peace because all I ever had to be was myself

and I damn sure am good at that.

I am my own perfect woman.

Therapy pt. 2

I walk into therapy like I walk into court.

Guilty until proven human.

Why are you here today? She asked.

Because I've been *"fine"* since forever.

Nobody sees me running for my life...

Nobody sees me starving...

For softness, for rest,

for a body that feels like home instead of a battlefield

I have to win every single day.

The addiction is not just drugs.

It's my need for control.

For perfection.

It's my bad habits.

My routine.

I lost myself somewhere in between

too much or not enough.

I call it discipline,

she calls it a disorder.

Why do I believe that suffering is somehow sacred?

Maybe because I watched the women around me

give until they were hollow and call it devotion.

They wore exhaustion like honor.

They smiled through grief and still made dinner.

I told myself joy was something you had to earn by bleeding first.

Relapse is not failure, she said.

It's a language your body still speaks when it's scared.

You're allowed to start over again as many times as you need.

That's the beauty of every day.

Some days healing looks like breakfast.

It looks like a good shower.

It looks like movement.

It looks like laughter in the middle of a breakdown

because something in you still believes

in light even when the room is dark.

It looks like not running from fear but sitting with it instead.

Some days healing looks like craving chaos and choosing calm.

I have a little girl I need to take care of.

I'm trying so fucking hard just to show up for myself...

Who you're becoming will thank you for showing up.

She's already so proud of you.

She wants you to keep going.

She wants you to give yourself a chance

to see how good it can get.

Harmony

Just her

and the echo of a man who never stayed long enough

to teach her how to love without disappearing.

She learned love from books and podcasts,

music and daydreams;

and moments she wished

someone would come home

and explain it all...

A man.

Big and masculine.

Some days soft and a gentleman,

other days rough and strong.

I've seen him in demolition.

I've seen him build a home.

I've seen him protect his own.

I know what power he holds.

How do I let him hold me?

How do I let him lead me?

How do I trust that this time will be different?

How do I let go of that idea of love?

How do I know when I'm ready

to hold on to a love that won't mislead me

or leave me at the mercy of uncertainty?

Go dance.

dance on a new idea.

Let it rock your world.

Stop begging the past to come back and explain itself.

Surrender to something new, let it excite you.

Trust your knowing and listen to your own heart beat.

Let leadership be love, not control.

You'll know you're ready when fear turns into faith.

When you don't want to run, you want to stay

and embrace him like he embraces you.

Let partnership be rhythm.

Perfection doesn't exist here.

Just you and me,

trying to stay open

and locked in…

At the same time.

What if this whole thing is about being brave enough to start over again and again and again…

20 something

Hey you,

I know you met the most broken,

yet the strongest version of yourself in your twenties.

I know how love humbled you, love humiliated you.

Love also uplifted you and carried you this far.

I know who you're becoming

challenges everything you stand for

but my favorite thing about you is your heart;

and the way you choose to see the world.

Your perspective is refreshing.

You find joy in being a blessing to others.

Your laughter is infectious, it lights up the entire room.

You are the most unapologetic person I know.

I love that you're becoming exactly who your inner child needed.

Your curiosity, your fearlessness, and bravery is unwavering.

You do things even when you're scared.

You know exactly what you want from life.

You feed all of your desires, big and small.

You disciplined yourself to wake up with the sun.

You dance when you eat and sing in the shower.

You are the most beautiful without makeup.

Little you is in awe of you!

So if there's anything I learned...

Its that years go by fast so don't be in a hurry.

You don't want to miss your own life.

You're not supposed to have it all figured out

but when you finally decide,

I hope you choose a life that entices, invigorates and inspires you.

Do it all while you're young and hot

because once you reach grown and sexy,

that comes with more responsibilities,

respect and a reason to take your ass home.

An Unapologetic Life

Let them wonder about you.

Let them ask questions about who you once were.

Let them not recognize who you're becoming.

It's okay if they don't understand where you are on your journey.

You don't owe anyone an explanation.

If I'm being real, I can't apologize for this.

I'm not sorry for what I'm about to say,

I'm not sorry for the things I've done.

I live a life with no regrets.

I can proudly say I did whatever I wanted

despite what the people said.

I broke their rules and wrote my own.

I let the world define success.

I'll choose the life that I love best.

I speak with purpose,

I move with presence,

I love without apology.

Do you know the braver you are, the luckier you get?

Do you know what it's like to follow your own lead?

The grace of god is my speed.

Free yourself from who they told you to be.

Can't ask for directions from people
who would never know what it's like to walk in your shoes.

Find your own way…

As crazy,

as outlandish,

as far fetched,

as weird

as it may be…

Go all out.

Take the risk.

Shoot your shot.

You only got one chance.

Bet on yourself.

You have to understand that nobody is you

and that is your superpower.

That is your key to an unapologetic life.

You're not going to like me.

I might not be who you're used to.

I know it takes a wild woman to welcome destruction.

But what seems like delusion to you,

is faith to me.

Faith Over Fear

How many times do we have to experience endings until we no longer fear change?

Possibly never.

However, we learn to embrace it more courageously.

Faith allows you to trust direction without needing to understand it.

The Unprofessional

They call me unprofessional –
But maybe that's the point.
I know it's not traditional.
I'm not here to master the map
or follow your directions.
I'm here to get lost in it.

A student of life, always.

I wander without needing arrival,
I learn by touch instead of title.
I don't want to perform knowing –
I want to feel discovery.
I've spent lifetimes coloring outside the lines,
undoing what the world told me to be.
I'd rather be the fool who learns,
than the master who's forgotten wonder.
If that makes me unprofessional,
Then I'll wear the title like a crown.

Dancing In The Reign

Sunday Service

Grand rising,

It's Sunday and I'm here to sing my psalms.

This is my service to the people.

This is my gift from the lord.

I will begin by giving thanks.

Thanks to the most high,

who has been my salvation

in my darkest nights and in all my glory.

Thanks for everything.

God I ask that you guide and protect

those suffering from poverty, hunger, and disease.

May you put war to rest and our hearts at peace.

May you heal thy healers and thy healers heal thee.

Shall we not forget who is he.

For he has risen, reigns and always right.

Shall we not forget who is he.

For he is our one and only savior.

He is king.

God is good

God is great

God is grand

Purple Reign

Blue tears and red wine,

purple reign down on me.

I don't need your umbrella,

I wanna feel everything.

When it hurts so good,

I call that purple pain.

This is dancing in the reign.

The Holy Grail

Water is the sign.

Water is the reign.

Water is the breakthrough.

Water is the main.

Water is the fuel.

Water is cool.

Water is the force.

Water is the source.

Water is baptising.

Water is life.

Good Mourning

Not a good mourning without a good cry.

Not a good mourning without a long sigh.

Not a good mourning without a goodbye.

Goodbye to your good mourning.

I don't want to cry anymore.

I don't want to find myself on the bathroom floor.

I don't want every day to feel like war.

Today, I decided I will lift me up

higher than the day before

because I knew it had to be something more.

Something more than this grief.

Something more than a hopeless dream.

I can't keep drowning in an endless sea…

I'm not the woman you used to know,

I'm a woman who knows how to rise.

Joy

I've been finding joy in the little things.

I enjoy watching the kids play outside,

losing track of time;

not realizing how life passes you by.

I'm still a kid at heart.

When did I start taking life so seriously?

Trying to balance work and play.

Since when did the fun turn into business?

Growing up is weird.

You outgrow everything.

Since when did I not fit in my favorite blue jeans anymore?

Since when did I outgrown my own place

and needed more space?

Since when did I start to consider myself a grown woman?

Then it comes a time in life

when being grown really just means

returning back to your inner child.

Returning back to nature,

returning back to adventure and freedom.

Since when did we build our wall of

discipline and responsibilities

so high we forgot what having fun looks like?

We forgot how our passions were fueled.

We forgot what inspires us the most.

Since when did we lose our sense of wonder?

Since when did we stop being so curious?

Since when did we outgrow what started all of this?

I still find joy in the little things.

Road trips and beach days,

tanlines and sunshine,

a good ol' walk in the park,

dancing in the rain,

bike rides,

ice cream.

On the swing just swinging

Laughing with God.

Realizing the beauty in simplicity.

Too many full circle, ah-ha moments.

All I had to do was think

and it all becomes one in the same.

Life is humorous

and most of all,

Unpredictable.

Karma & Destiny

I can't tell if they're best friends or fraternal twins.

Definitely have their own identity

because they show up differently.

But you'll never see one without the other.

Karma isn't a bitch, she's a mirror.

Reflecting back to you;

Do you like what you see?

The rewards you reap

from diving deep,

down to where it all started.

This is the only way to pay your karmic debt.

Karma likes to spin the block a few times

just to make sure we're moving like we know better this time.

Karma comes full circle

just so you can realize it was your destiny.

It takes destiny to unfold to see how our karma plays out…

Wait till destiny shows her face.

Then we'll understand what karma made us go through.

What's meant for you will always be your destiny.

But the route you take to arrive

at your destination is your karma.

If you don't know where you're going, every road will lead to nothing.

.

Direction over speed.

Wednesday

If you read too closely,

You'll find a girl like Wednesday.

Dark, witty, and twisted in a fantasy of her own.

– because it's not all love and light.

In fact, I love rainy days when the skies are grey.

Darkness isn't the absence of light,

It's where I write my best work.

The only color you'll find

is when my pen bleeds red or blue.

The world has their thoughts of me

but I think none of you.

What is normal to the spider,

is chaos to the fly.

The tsunami is near –

But sovereignty is not a storm to fear.

The reign is mine and could be yours too

If you dare to dance in the shadows as I do.

Tsunami Warning

The reign is coming.

I see a wave larger than life.

While the people run mad, I don't fret.

I bring out the ark I've built.

I invite the animals.

I am not afraid of lions or bears.

I wish I could bring them all.

On board are members only.

God is the captain of this ship.

I follow my moral compass.

Lighthouses are a sign of hope.

At last, we get to sail.

Off to the promiseland;

Where the sun shall rise again.

Members Only

Lord, please guide me.

Can't always have it my way.

I know whatever you say goes

like a flower that rose,

I'll rise if you say so.

Save my soul.

You're the only one

who knows.

Who chose;

Chosen one.

Real one.

Reach one.

Teach one.

Love one.

Know one.

Bless one.

If you know one,

become one.

One of a kind;

I'm one of them ones.

The last ones laughing.

Last ones standing.

But the last ones made first.

You just had to be there.

Purging,

soul searching,

marching…

Members only.

March madness.

March forward.

March band.

March miles.

March child.

March again...

Past Lives

Who were you before you got here?

How many lives have you lived?

Did you take the time to let go of who you were then?

with them, over there, on that side?

Can't bring that over here.

The old paradigm is outdated.

Bring your blessings, leave the rest.

Welcome to your new life.

Love Is King

The Journey Home

A sense of being here or there unsettles me.

Longing for a home I can't seem to know where it exists.

A foreign place or is it you that can bring me this?

We travel far and wide;

only to be brought back to each other's eyes.

Home is where the heart is.

Forgive me for the times my mind

and heart were in two different places.

I'm just wandering, still trying to find my way.

Still trying to define what love is to me.

Don't mind if I go, don't mind if I stay.

It's all love, that's a promise I can keep.

Come home. We love you here.

Even if it's just me.

Where Have You Been?

I can't wait to meet you.

You never feel so far away.

You feel intimate and familiar.

Though I don't know your name

or what you look like,

I know how you smell.

Indescribable and delicious.

Where have you been?

who knows…

I hope you find what you've been longing for.

I hope it doesn't take forever and a day

for our ends to meet.

I'll be waiting till the end of time

for our paths to align.

All else feels out of place.

You're the only thing I'm sure of.

Please stop testing my patience.

It's safe here, my love.

Stars Align

I met you somewhere before the stars had names.

Where silence was song and fire had wings.

You carried the sun in your chest and I, the sea in mine.

I saw myself in your fire

and you saw yourself in my flood.

We were mirrors turned inside out.

My moon was your shadow,

your light was my longing.

You run so you can find truth.

I wait so I can feel it.

You give me room to wander,

I give you space to land.

Somewhere in between

the arrow and the ocean;

We are learning to love in a language only the sky remembers.

So let's not name it.

Let's live it, not control it.

But flow and blaze

and build something real

from the wild of us.

Polarities

I see love in possibility,

you see love in presence.

I swim towards forever,

you lay the stones beneath my feet.

You are the hearth,

I am the horizon.

You show me how to stay,

I show you how to soar.

Somewhere between roots and wings,

between prayer and passion;

We've made a sacred kind of magic.

Untamed

I've kissed a wolf, hugged a bear and fed a lion.

I am no stranger to the wild life.

But if it's one thing for sure,

none of them can be tamed.

You've got to accept the raw,

honest and wild nature of it all.

Love is Free

Some people spend lifetimes exploring dead ends,
carrying dead weight and attached to expired relationships.
It comes to a point
where if you really love someone,
you got to give them their freedom.
You got to liberate yourself too.
You've got to choose you.
Avoid roads that lead to nothing.
Let me tell you something…

Let love go.

Let love go run.

Let love go have fun.

Let love get lost.

Let love call you back.

Let love find home,

even if home isn't where you're at.

Let love roam.

Let love just be a poem.

Let love be love because love is free.

Love is grace

and sometimes love has a different face.

I hope you recognize love in its many shapes.

Understanding love, knowing love makes mistakes.

Knows love probably made a couple wrong turns.

Knows love is just living and that's how we learn.

But love is patient and only love can wait…

And she's waiting for you to love yourself.

Consciousness Awakening

Be the embodiment of love.

Move that energy forward.

Share it with the world

because it raises humans

and we rise by lifting each other.

Nothing is accidental,
everything is on purpose.

Love is King

We have the whole world right here.

Look at all of the lights.

We got a big room with city views.

Press me up against the windows.

Let's put on a good show.

Who cares who views.

Can't tell me nothing.

This is our homecoming.

Treat it like royalty

because family means everything.

In too deep, how could you even pull out?

Let love reign.

You should wear a starry crown because love is king.

Our name has a nice ring.

I think we got a sweet thing.

All eyes on us when we walk in the room.

Don't listen to what they say,

you know I'm unapologetic about you.

Who cares who views.

I love it when you come to town.

Call me, let's go out.

Let's go show this off.

They ain't never seen

a man who loves his queen

as much as you love reina.

We have the whole world right here.

Look at all of the lights.

We got a big room with city views.

Press me up against the windows.

Let's put on a good show.

Who cares who views.

You got me like this

and I don't usually write back.

But I'll put your name in a tatt.

Red ink cause I'm really blood about you.

Don't listen to what they say about us,

you know I'm unapologetic about you.

Who cares who views.

Who cares when it's just me and you.

Let love reign because love is king.

Queen & Him

The day I met him for the first time…again.

We had a run away kind of love.

A love that is grim and dies in the end.

We heard sirens while we made love

but that didn't stop us.

We were too locked in.

It was him for me and I his queen.

If my man was fighting some unholy war,

I would be behind him.

I'd be right there to remind him of his strength.

My lion heart has enough pride to believe;

because you don't know my man.

You don't know him.

Hopeless Romantic

I wonder about you.

I wander for you.

I let my thoughts wonder to places I shouldn't go.

I let my body wander to places I shouldn't go.

I shouldn't go but still,

I stretched my hand out to reach you.

Thinking you would love me back the same.

Foolish of me,

hopeful of me,

curious of me,

to chase after a hopeless dream.

Curiosity killed the cat every time she wandered too far off…

Into the deep end…

I wonder about you.

I wander for you.

I know I shouldn't go there;

but still I go…

Hoping you would meet me there too.

You cannot save people,
only love them where they are.

Guns & Roses 2

When you tell me you're making your way back home,

where is home to you when you're not with me?

Where does your heart wander to when you're feeling free?

How can I believe the things you say to me,

when I know how sticky sweet can be.

Behind closed doors, secretly sliming me.

Next time I see you, I love how you lie to me.

You say you're the man for me

but you don't love yourself, honestly.

Turning me into a woman I know I shouldn't be.

I hate that we let it get here.

I wish you loved me like you promised.

My broken heart is an ugly girl.

She wants you to feel the pain you caused her.

She has roses that'll make you bleed.

She has tricks up her sleeve,

wicked schemes, petty things.

My wandering heart is feeling free.

But do my selfish desires truly bring me peace?

I know it is wrong of me to

step outside of the woman I should be.

I like it better when you're away from me.

I can do bad all by myself.

Fucking leave me alone.

You don't know what love is so you blame me.

Think I'm moving shady, so you shame me.

I'm tired of all the back and forth.

Since when were we against one another?

It feels like I'm in competition with my lover.

Like who can cause the most damage…

Put your guns down babe,

roses die on their own.

A Goddamn Villain

We're all the villain in somebody's story.

If I am yours, I hope you tell it like I said it.

I meant every word when I said,

"I just might break your heart."

Even after that I'm still your love

because nobody could ever play my part.

Did you forget I have the key?

I've unlocked levels soul deep.

How could you ever forget a woman like me?

This ain't a fucking love story.

You were scared of your own shadow.

You'd tell me I'm doing too much when I would shine my light.

I told you I'd hold your hand in the dark but you didn't trust me

when I said *"I'm not a woman for the faint of heart."*

I am a storm dressed in art.

In unlocking your truths,

Does this make me the villain in your story?

because I broke your heart trying to crack the code.

Kiss It Better

I wonder if she knows all the meanings of your tattoos.

I wonder if she can put that smile on your face like I do.

I wonder if this is what you planned all along.

I wonder if you built your happy home.

Are you happy there?

Tell me about her…

What is she willing to do?

Would she go to war like I would for you?

I wonder if she wonders too…

About the love that came before the love that is.

Does it hurt?

The way you left me out in the rain.

The way you lied on my name.

The way you played me like your favorite key.

The way you turned me blue.

Does it hurt you?

If so, does she kiss it better?

Like I Do

Why does it feel like such a crime to love you?

Keeping it lowkey to protect us.

Keeping you close cause if they find out about a love like this,

they're gonna want to kill us both.

They hate the smile you put on my face.

But I must say, I love who I am with you.

If only they knew… who you are when you're next to me.

They'll never see you like I do.

When they question your love for me,

do you curse my name?

or do you tell them how I bring out the best in you?

Flex my love.

Show them something you believe in.

Give them another reason…

To think I'm crazy for loving you.

To think I'm crazy for loving you.

They'll never see you like I do.

Nights In Paris

I've never been to France

but I have been in love.

So in love I became Paris.

The city of romance.

I romanticized every night

with wine and roses,

red lipstick and white sheets.

Admiring the city lights.

All we need is a boat ride

and a date night at the opera.

Dinner was amazing.

I hope you're enjoying your night in love.

Pardon my French but if I could, I would scream

'Je t'aime' from the Eiffel tower.

This is poetry, you said

and so, I wrote…

This Isn't About You

Every step I take in the opposite direction of you,

reminds me of my power.

How brave of me to walk away from you like that

when I wrote you into my story.

I guess I was only a chapter in yours.

Now to go on, out into the world, alone once again.

Yet this time, I will not play small or sell myself short.

I know better now.

So I put away the hoodie you gave me last October.

I burned every letter ever written by you.

The photographs of you and I are cleared from my gallery.

You are the last of my old things.

But this isn't about you.

It's about me grieving who I once was

and writing a new story.

French Exit

I'm not a woman for the faint of heart.

We will go on walks in the park, visit museums,

we will hold hands at the top of the world.

I will kiss you in French,

I will kiss you in all your favorite places

so that you can't go back to them without the thought of me

dancing in your mind.

I will destroy you in the most beautiful way;

and when I finally leave,

you will understand why

romance is red.

Traveling

Dear you,

You know who you are.

Remember you told me I should follow my north star?

That my silver lining won't ever lead me astray

even if my dreams are wild, I should just 'go for it'

Thank you for believing in me that much.

Traveling is my favorite thing to do.

I'm on a one way flight.

I don't know when I'll ever settle for my life.

Everything is still in motion…

I'll write you when I land

just to tell you I made it safe.

It's been 3 years since we last spoke…

Crazy how we missed out on so much of each other's lives.

By the time you read this,

We'll be in two different places.

We just aren't in alignment anymore.

No love lost, life just goes on…

On to the next chapter…

I had to let go of a lot, including you.

It hurts me most but I know love isn't possessive.

I seen the way you looked out the window

as if you're wondering

who's watching the stars on the other side.

Maybe one day you'll get the chance to meet them…

So here's your chance…

Thank you for sharing your time with me.

I don't know how long I will write to you

or if this will be the last time.

But you know this is how I find my way.

I pray you find yours.

My dearest, I beg of you… go for it.

I like you happy, you deserve that much.

Even if that means letting go of everything you've ever known.

I know you will meet with grace and glory.

They will hug you and remind you when discourage arises,

that sometimes bravery feels like fear;

but their kindness eases the change.

It breathes new life into us.

Honestly, I wouldn't truly love you if I let you stay.

Love wants more for you,

what's best for you.

Even if that means departure…

For now or forever.

Sincerely, somebody that you used to know

The key to alignment is listening to the voice within instead of the noise around you.

The Fisherman & The Pisces

As above, so below…

He watched me dance

on the edge of two worlds.

Every movement pulled him

like the moon pulls the sea.

Two souls divided by the ocean,

yet bound by something none could chart.

His anchor met my wandering heart.

As I paint a dream I've yet to live.

His hands wait where dreams meet the shore.

How many lives have we touched before?

This one feels different…

I surrendered to him, the sea,

and the tides of fate.

A bond the heavens reconciled.

True love becomes destiny's child.

Thank you, next.

They never loved you.

They only loved you when

you never made them question themselves.

Once it's finally over,

I hope you don't call it heartbreak.

I hope you call it awakening.

Because they were never meant to be yours.

They were positioned to mirror you

until you remember yourself.

And when you remember,

they don't know who you are anymore…

But this isn't your ending,

It's your upgrade.

It's sad because some people can't move on with you.

They're written as

the reason you left.

One Life, Many Dreams

You've said goodbye to versions of yourself
that once dreamed many dreams.
You let go of the wild and wondrous ''what ifs''
In order to choose something steady and real.
I want you to know, this is not a weakness or settling.
This is what courage looks like when
you make decisions for yourself.
You chose to see how good it can get.
Love doesn't always feel like fireworks or a fairytale.
Sometimes it's soft and quiet.
But it should always feel effortless.
Love makes you feel seen and safe without having to perform.
That is real and rare;
And the real magic happens when
you choose a life that feels in alignment for you.

The Elephant In The Room Is You

Healing

Healing is a sacred experience. It demands honesty.

Forthcoming pain, pain teaches us to persevere.

Perseverance requires strength.

Strength reminds us of our ability to hold weight.

Push it. Lift it. Release it.

The art of resilience rather than resistance.

Pain is our teacher.

If you listen closely, it will tell you where it hides

and how the only way to heal is to surrender.

Sometimes we get lucky to have a moment

of relief so we can catch our breath.

But it's not up to us to decide when it's over.

It both fascinates and terrifies me

how fast life pushes us to get over things.

The ever changing reality is that

we cannot hold onto anything for too long

before another wave comes.

We're not granted enough time and space

to hold onto anything longer than life allows

It pains us most that we can't hold ourselves

and each other on our own time.

It's always divine timing we must trust in.

When was the last time you were able

to sit under the trees and talk to the sky

without feeling rushed or pushed into the next direction?

We always have somewhere to be.

I'm trying to be where my feet land me.

I'm trying to be in my body.

I'm trying to be at heart.

I'm trying to be still

even when movement races at the speed of light.

I'm trying to pace myself

even when my patience is being tested

because I can't control the rhythm of my blues

or the cadence of life.

Many hours spent in silence in communication with God.

An omnipresent being who provides

direction and clarity when sought.

It'll pass you by if you're not present enough.

God's voice is heard by those who aren't

distracted by the noise of the world.

It's our responsibility to not let anything outside of us,

rush us out of a moment with God.

Love is patient and kind enough to wait

on the faithful to position themselves

to hear the word and understand the message.

Only then will we be delivered.

I must thank pain for how it humbles me

and stills my rushing heart.

A reminder that healing isn't linear but

God meets us wherever we are in our journey.

Grand Theft

Tried to rob me of my blessings.

Tried to rob me of my delight.

Tried to rob me of my successes.

Tried to rob me of my divine right.

But you can't rob me of my pen.

This is my sword and it is sharpened.

I'll write it all into existence.

I took it to a level you can't reach me at.

You can't rob me of this grandeur,

you can only be a bystander.

Rob them of their pleasure of theft.

Withhold them from the kingdom.

The trouble they cause recoils onto themselves.

Their violence comes down on their own heads.

The energy you sent is being returned to you.

How Many Real Friends?

There's really no friends in the game
I think I learned that now.
Just cause everybody's out,
doesn't mean I gotta stay down.
I'm not playing around.
Y'all so played out.
The ball is in my court, I gotta be a good sport.
Can't let myself fall short over a couple fall outs.
I would call you out
but nah, look at all the shit you do for attention.
You don't deserve a mention.
Crazy when you act out of character.
It's embarrassing.
You got them asking…
Is that your friend?
Because a real one would never.
Reasons why we fell off.
I think it was better off…
Go play with someone else.

The Elephant
& The Phoenix

You should sit and read a book
about how the elephant in the room is you
and why you should take the time to acknowledge
your big ignorant self instead of running the streets
like a wild animal.
I stopped going out on the weekends when
I realized nobody is celebrating; they're just coping.
Drinking to forget the week but only the weak fill voids.
Dancing to loud music instead of spending hours in silence.
I used to mistake noise for joy.
The crowd for connection.
But that isn't the vibe I'm going for.
Your fun is avoidance dressed as confidence;
not realizing your choices have consequences.
Eventually, you pay the price.
So I hope you make smart choices
and choose to become the phoenix instead of the elephant.

Close

Friends are close but the enemies are closer.

Acting like they ride for you but really they're a poser.

Wanna get close just to know where it hurts most.

Make jokes on a post

but there's truth in laughter.

That could be you, how dare you laugh at her.

Ain't shit funny when the tables turn.

I had to cut you off.

That's a bridge I thought I'd never burn.

Called you my friend but I kept you too close.

So close you thought you could tell my story better than I can.

So close I slept next to the opposition.

So close you thought you can take my position.

You know me too well.

I thought it was safe to share.

Safe to keep you near.

You said you loved it here.

How could you do it with so much grace

and throw it right in my face.

Never thought it would be you.

You're too familiar to me.

More than friends,

I called you my family.

It be your own people

that'll do you so lethal.

I'll take the knife right out my back

and cut you right off.

Devil's Paradise

Know this world of materialism isn't all yours.

This world roams many devils in many forms.

I met a few and they drive Benz's.

I met a few and they look expensive.

Never cared about their hot wheels or big bills

if that means I gotta sell my soul.

This world is cold

especially to the godly folks.

Watch your desires.

It might take you higher,

but the devil is a good liar.

He'll deceive you into believing that the world is yours.

This world roams many devils in many forms.

I met a few and they never are what they seem.

I met a few and they have tricks up their sleeve.

The type to come off as good,

but it's never as good as it seems.

Question everything.

The devil is a liar.

The devil will deceive.

Gotta rise above this plane.

Gotta rise above this game.

Gotta rise above these bills.

Gotta only seek God's change.

The devil is in the details.

Demons

Perhaps, I could be doing better things with my time
than drinking wine and spilling it on the lines.
Can't tell if I'm crying or laughing over wasted times.
I can only attend my own pity party.
Only I can finish what I started
so let me clean up the mess I made.

Oh, what a mess I made trying to dig up your grave.
Trying to resurrect what I thought was dead to me.
I thought I slayed these demons.
I thought I put these thoughts to rest.
But there's no rest for you and your wicked ways
if you keep on feeding the beast.
But I knew what it was when I signed up.

Ain't nothing new under the sun.

I know all your dirt.

I know where it's rooted from.

I know all your hurt.

You've become so transparent to me;

Ain't nothing you could do that could spook me.

I know love and I know lust.

I know what it means when texts go green.

I know karma and I know her best friend destiny.

No more tricks and treats.

Can't give them another drink.

No more wine and spirits;

it's all parasitic behavior.

It's time to slay those demons.

Reaper

The seeds have been sown, they have all grown.

Look at the fields, they are ready for harvest.

Thanks to the work the people have put in.

And you like to reap the benefits of their labor;

low, down, dirty, shameful behavior.

I know how you try to make it work in your favor.

Not one to guide, nor guard or keep.

Only to take, to cut, to reap.

They may follow blindly but not I.

I see right through your sheep clothing. I know your kind.

I know a good shepherd when I see one, but I see none in you.

You love to play devil's advocate.

You are no keeper of light.

Only a shadow that walks at night.

Someday you will finally reap what you sow

and face the weight of all you know.

Rumor Has It

Rumor has it and they can keep it…

I won't beg to be chosen or seen.

Believe them if you will.

I know who I am, I know my truth.

I stand tall in my skin.

I give up trying to prove my integrity.

I give up trying to convince you of my nobility.

I just am and that is all.

A Moment of Silence

Why is silence so awkward?

What comfort is found in all the noise?

Why is silence so embarrassing?

As if noise hides all of our flaws

Why is silence always broken?

As if noise fixes it all…

Homework

I know you have wounds that are bleeding.

I know you have trauma that is leaking.

I know you have an ego that's speaking.

I know you have an inner child that's screaming.

I know how it can be triggering.

I know you have pain that needs healing.

On the other side of your pain and fear is courage.

The courage to accept what's been hurting you

and use it as your muse to reinvent a greater version of you.

Emotional intelligence is the art of self mastery.

Grant yourself the grace to feel what you feel

but make sure you make your way back to peace.

Through discomfort only then can we become good comforters.

Let's not sweep our problems under the rug.

Let's not ignore the elephant in the room.

I know you have wounds that are bleeding.

I know you have trauma that is leaking.

I know you have an ego that's speaking.

I know you have an inner child that's screaming.

I know how it can be triggering.

I know you have pain that needs healing.

Nobody wants to do their homework

but that's the key to earning a degree in self mastery.

Not only are you healing yourself,

you're healing your ancestors from patterns of destruction.

You're healing future bloodlines to move in divine love.

You can't coach anybody for greatness and be nice, a good coach will challenge you.

Forgiveness

I hope you sat with yourself long enough to find forgiveness

to understand that life comes and goes as it pleases;

and we have no control over the seasons

or whatever is the reason,

what happened, happened.

It's a new day.

I gotta clear my heart from yesterday's pain.

I can't carry it with me.

I can't take it too personal.

It's not all mine to hold.

So I'll hold you accountable for you and yours.

I hope you sat with yourself long enough to find forgiveness.

I've been sitting here counting all the reasons why.

'Why?' is the big question.

Why did you move like that?

Why did I go about my day like that?

Why did we cause so much pain?

Perhaps, it was our own to hold.

Instead, we threw it at each other in vain.

So let's not hold it against one another.

We both made mistakes.

We both had our faults.

I never wanted to be on two different sides

but there's two sides to the same coin

so I guess we both have our own truths.

I'll let you live in yours.

Let me live in mine.

Maybe it's not meant to see eye to eye.

Maybe it's not meant to align.

It's okay, I forgive you.

Granting Grace

I know you tend to self sabotage and ruin things

before they ruin you.

Before it has a chance to run its course

because you want to finish writing the story.

The end terrifies you so much that

you decide to put matters in your own hands

and write the happily ever after that you desire…

But the truth is…

You don't get to decide God's plan.

What's for you, will be for you.

Let it all work out, graciously.

Me, You & Our Sun

Down to Earth

The truth is…

A lot of this is ego driven.

Do the views get you high?

Do the hearts make you feel loved?

Nobody posts the raw shit

So maybe I should talk about it.

The blood, the mud, the rage and the fire.

Maybe then it'll be respected more.

Through my humility and humanity.

Maybe then I could remind you what life is like

when you're alone in your room with all the scary things.

I don't think we've ever been this real.

Face to face with big truths.

Present in this human experience.

God is more interested in your character than your comfort.

For The Love of God

I heard my calling and God said…

Arise my darling,

good things ahead.

Keep your eyes open,

keep your head up,

keep your heart with all vigilance.

Diligence will take you far.

You shall reach the promise land.

Your kingdom will be on earth.

You will not have to die to see another dimension.

Prayer is your transportation and it will drive you.

So you will see the goodness of God in the land of the living.

So I rose in the dark.

I had to meet God right in my pain.

He called me and I had to say his name.

God,

I'm living a life that confuses the enemy

Let the enemy wonder…

How did all the storms I put her through,

not keep her from pursuing the dream?

By the grace of God

By the grace of God

By the grace of God

Sunday

Once again,

grand rising

Sunday reminds me to stop and smell the roses.

Sometimes I talk to the sky.

I breathe its air.

We exchange life.

I tell the heavens…

Will you let me make the sun my own?

For my love shines bright

Can the ocean be mine?

I know her blues

Can I raise your mountains?

Can I call them my daughters?

I feel at home in the embrace of your nature.

Partner For Life

Women either bleed or hold the smallest version of you for life.

Her timeless ocean of blood is the source of all creation.

Here death and resurrection are fully honored.

Her womb is also the tomb in which she will enlighten him.

Welcome him into a world where her powers of transformation

will help him slay his demons.

So because of a woman,

he knows God.

We are one.

In cocreation,

the ego is born.

A Star Is Born

Long before a star was born,

I've dreamed of your eyes…

You found me here

learning my lesson.

Waiting for my blessing.

I never knew it'd have your face.

Love called me.

Love demanded me.

This is where love landed me

and said this is the plan, no plan B.

Ready or not,

this is my karma to hold.

Teach me how to hold joy.

Father stretch my hands.

I leave it up to you;

The way you trust me with your life.

Another Life

Because of a woman I know God.
I saw what God could do when he gave me you.
Forgive me please, for not being ready to receive
such a blessing you are.

My body is so sacred.
You showed me just how creative I can really be.
Right when I thought I didn't have it in me, it's in too deep.
Forgive me, for sending you back to spirit.
I wish I was ready.

I wish I chose you like you chose me.
Like my mother chose to keep me.
I wish I could keep you.
I wish I didn't feel you.
I feel you from the inside out
trying to make a home out of me.
I can't recognize my body.
You're taking a hold on me.
Sorry I couldn't hold you.

Sorry I miscarried you.

Maybe I'm too weak.

Maybe I'm too selfish.

Maybe now isn't the time…

9 months later…

I still wonder about you.

I wonder if you've forgiven me yet.

I wonder if you found another place to call home.

I wonder what's the point in missing you…

In passing you, a part of me died too.

The biggest ego death, reality check.

I promise the next time we make it this far,

You'll get to meet daddy.

You'll get to come home.

We'll get to call you by name.

You'll have the best birthday ever

Bleeding Love

For the life I never got to hold…

I whispered your name many times.

I thought the world would finally make sense with you in it.

But silence…

A pain so deep it had no language.

Just a heartbeat.

Your name turned red.

I bled in a white dress.

Somedays I wonder who you would've been.

What your laugh might've sounded like.

If you would've had my smile or his eyes.

But I do know this…

you were real and you were mine.

Midwife

Dear woman, know that you were born for this.

Dear wife, know that you have made magic.

Dear mother, I see God in you.

I know I am something of that nature.

Something transformational, something divine.

Someone who knows grace, someone great.

I am a midwife.

Bringing forth all of the most wildest dreams.

Birthing them through the portal we call woman.

I could show you what it looks like to believe in yourself.

To anchor you back to self when the experiences we face become bigger than life.

Keep pushing through.

The Veil

The veil is lifting.

Everything done in the dark always comes to light.

All my love and devotion will be dedicated to you.

Somewhere between a dream and the becoming.

Heavy is the head that wears the crown.

But only you know how to lift it

and still see me as your honor.

Your truth is safe with me.

Is my truth safe with you?

Are we free to be ourselves?

Would you recognize me

time and time again?

Would you choose me and only me

over and over again?

The veil between what is

and what aches to be seen.

Trusting in godspeed.

What a mystery.

God, only you can get me like this.

Wide open and exposed.

Revealing my treasure and my truth.

Sandalwood and gold,

myrrh and rose.

You must be Godsent.

I can tell by your aura.

I can tell by your grace.

I can tell by the way you get on your knees and praise.

I can tell by the way you lift your queen even on her worst days.

I am blessed to be kissed by you.

Metamorphosis

You changed, they said.

You used to show up like this and now you don't.

What happened to you?

What happened to me is that I've grown.

I've grown up so much, you can hardly recognize me.

But I'm still the same girl.

With better boundaries,

with better communication,

with better understanding,

with better awareness.

No, it doesn't make me better than you;

but it does make me above a lot of the shit we used to do.

I learned how to pivot when life demanded.

Years go by so fast, how grown up are you?

I can tell by the things you choose to engage in.

You haven't changed one bit.

Complacency frightens me.

I've never been that comfortable.

I'd feel like a fool if I didn't take the chance

to become better than who I was or who I am.

Change requires a leap of faith.

I'm so glad I jumped timelines.

Now I know where to draw the line

between wanting more and settling.

Meet Me Here

These days I don't care to be seen.

I enjoy hibernation.

I enjoy being in my own world.

I don't follow the crowd because the crowd is lost.

Lost in the thrill of it all. I don't follow the hype.

Too many demons in the mix so I stay out of it.

I hate the club.

I enjoy the simple things in life.

I wanna sit still.

I wanna listen to the birds.

I wanna swim good.

I wanna sit by the fire.

I wanna hike mountains.

I wanna read books and drink tea.

I enjoy the simple things.

If you're looking for me,

I'm somewhere connected to spirit.

Come meet me here.

Keep the Faith

If you're looking for something to believe in…

Let me hold you.

Let me hold your worries.

Let me hold your weary heart.

Let me hold your aching bones.

Let me hold your anxiousness.

Let me hold your loneliness.

Let me help you carry the weight of the world.

I know the load is heavy.

I know how you break your back.

I know how you wish someone had your back.

Let me hold you.

This is a safe space.

A place you can keep your faith.

If you're looking for something to believe in,

can you believe in me?

Believe the prayers I sent.

Believe the blessings on their way.

I had to hold on.

I had to slow down.

I had to hold myself together.

This is how I built my strength.

This is how I know how to hold you

because I had to carry myself through.

I ain't even gon hold you.

Believe It

God gave me what my great grandmother lost.

I am a witness of his goodness.

I am a walking testimony.

God keeps all the records.

This is years in the making.

How could I not believe it?

When I am the one who stands tall in answered prayers.

"You are everything I ever dreamed of.

I want to be you when I grow up."

Love, mom

Inner Child

At some point I became my mother.

Or should I say… I met my daughter before we became two.

I guess we are one in the same.

When I think of her I see myself.

A young girl who is funny and so full of life.

Deserving of all the good things.

I try to protect her from the bad.

I worry about her when she's out too late.

I tell her not to fall in love too quickly.

I hold her like my very own,

indeed she is my very own.

I feed her, I bathe her,

I buy her books and teach her big words

like "accolades" and "ambiguity"

I comb her hair and tell her it's okay to cry if you want to.

We dance together when she feels lonely.

I remind her that I'm her best friend

and she doesn't need no other body.

I show her how to love hers.

We do face masks together and then smile in the mirror.

I tell her in the mirror that I am proud of her.

"We've come so far and look

at all the big girl things you do now."

I remind her that I'll always

hold her like this when she needs me.

I was not always this gentle with her.

I pray she forgives me for those years.

I was young and I didn't know how

to take good care like my mother did.

Your mother knows better now.

Closer than ever, skin to skin.

I rock you to sleep and wake up to you every day.

My Favorite Teacher

I know you want to be someone.
Whoever you become,
know that you came from love.
Even though you're a pain,
you're my greatest joy.

My favorite girl,
my sweet boy.
I want you to love your life.
The way I dedicated mine to you.
Do you know what it means when you
can't fight what's in your nature?
It means we were made for this.
But I could never call myself a professional.
Your mother has a lot to learn,
teach her.

Wise beyond your years.
Little do you know,
You are the rising sun.
Suddenly my heart is yours, little one.

Time Travelers

The woman with the big curly hair is my mother.

The man with the deep voice is my father.

The girl with the big dreamy eyes is my sister.

The boy with the sad smile is my brother.

We have lived many lives so we shall live on once more.

Solana,

Luna,

Star,

Pea,

we will be scattered and gathered.

We live to serve life,

as life serves us.

I live through my kids, my mother says.

It's like giving birth to myself over and over again.

When I see you, I see every generation before you.

Our ancestors run deep, we're time travelers.

The Grand Opera

The kids will sing from dusk to dawn.

Let's give them a good word.

Let's give them a good song.

Let's give them something

not only to chant, but to dance along.

The kids will sing on…

Let's give them a good word.

Let's give them a good song.

Let's give them justice.

Let's give them psalms.

The kids will sing everything we write.

The kids will sing loud;

they'll even sing of the silent night.

So with all of our might,

Let's give them a good word.

Let's give them a good song.

Let's remind them of their voices.

Let's show them how to use their instruments.

Voices echo through time.

Let's remind them the opera is beyond them…

The opera is grand.

Allow your inner child to trust the grown up that you are.

La Isla Del Encanto

Grand rising,

motherland.

On the island,

mi gente live on the tallest mountain

overlooking the countryside.

The roosters sing at dawn.

The horses run wild.

There are so many chickens.

I call the lambs by name.

The sun is beaming over the ocean.

The water is blue as day.

The palm trees sway.

I have family surrounding me.

I hug my grandfather;

which seems like the first and last time ever.

So I cherish this moment.

I laugh and I cry

tears of joy.

My heart is full.

It's refreshing to my spirit.

Thankful is an understatement.

Esto es una bendición.

Something In The Orange

Something in the orange breaks me open;

like the sun that never asked to set.

But it does anyway like a goodbye I didn't choose…

Orange butterfly.

Pumpkin, is that you?

The wind picks up.

The fall is here.

Orange leaves again…

I remember you every time.

You were the sun to me.

The color of home.

The color of love.

Something in the orange holds it all.

Don't ask how I am everywhere

yet, nowhere to be found.

Ask how you're just noticing...

The wind is able to reach every corner of the world.

Formless. Full of life. Invisible but powerful.

Carrying the voices of those whom we love.

A ghost. A traveler. Coming and going...

Me, You & Our Sun

The center of the universe is found in your eyes

– as the world spins round and round

and the moon goes through its phases,

we carry our sun between us like a tie that binds.

For the light in me recognizes the light in you

The Grand Finale: Sunset

Summer Rose

Last summer with you…

I fall in love with your eyes every time.
How do you make the world stop?
How do I explain to everyone what this is?
I'm not a science teacher but I know chemistry.
I know when magic is in the air.

Since day one
you've given me even more lust for life.
You added substance, you added color.
You remind me that life is well lived a little wild.
We roamed the city like it was ours.
We spent hours getting to know what it feels like
to be in love with someone who sees life as a thriller.

You sit with me on the highest mountain

and we watch the sunset over the land.

We feed the animals, we pray at the temple.

We sing at the karaoke bar downtown.

Everyday with you is my favorite.

Can we spend 50 more summers together?

I need you now and forevermore…

Sandcastle

Off the coast of wherever I am;

I sit in the sand.

I look out into the far distance.

I close my eyes.

I go into a trance.

All I hear is the ocean breeze

and suddenly time doesn't exist.

Here I am at the beach.

Just me and a day in my life.

Hoping the sandcastle I built

becomes more than a dream

and not just a vacation.

Please, make it a real destination.

I wanna call this castle home.

I watch as the sand slips through my fingers.

Wondering if anything is as real as it seems

or is life just a fucking beach?

Souvenir

Sometimes I wish I had no recollection of you.

I oh so badly wish you could be washed away from my memory.

No old photographs to reminisce on,

nothing to trigger the thought of you.

I don't even wanna hear 'our song' on the radio.

No trace of you,

no footsteps to follow.

No signs of you ever being here.

Just gone with the wind.

Maybe then my heart won't ache so bad

or maybe then it would ache even more

for a love just as profound as yours.

Who else knows the way the story goes

if they haven't lived it beside me, besides you…

Perhaps, the memories we made are

the most valuable thing we've created;

so let's create more art that reminds us

we're neither here nor there.

Art so timeless we can visit whenever we want.

Because art is a souvenir from

all the people and places we loved.

Fire Alarm

Two matches can start a fire
so I thought we were making smores,
I thought you would keep me warm.
Until you told me to feel the burn.
Like the orange sunset over the horizon,
it all became a blur.

I've seen your closed fists and open arms;
then I heard the fire alarms.
Too much smoke in the mirror
I don't recognize who I am.
How dare I let you smoke me like that.
I had you all fired up.
Shooting your shot.
I hope you miss it.

I hope you miss it.

Who thought it was a good idea to fight fire with fire?

Time flies when you're having fun.

All the fun is catching up to me;

None of it is pretty when the fire goes out

and this shit ain't lit no more.

Because even the sun sets in paradise.

I suppose it was my reminder to let myself burn to ashes

Just to rise again.

Love After Grief

I looked you in the face after you burned our house down.

I looked you in the face after you stabbed me in my back.

I looked you in the face after you sold my dream.

I looked you in the face after you killed my wife.

Not once did I choose violence.

Instead I chose distance and silence.

It still keeps me up at night;

Wondering…how dare you?

Or how dare I still choose love after grief.

Options

Weighing my options on this libra scale.

Not sure if the options will ever balance out.

Trying to figure out if it is worth playing for keeps

or is this the part where I should go now?

Trying to figure out how I can have my cake and eat it too

but they said I can't have the best of both worlds.

So how do I choose?

Can't be so afraid to lose.

Something has to give.

The grass is only green where you water it.

Somehow my generosity thinks I have enough

to pour into everyone's cup.

Wait til you find out you're not everyone's cup of tea.

Only then will you save some for yourself

and those who are deserving.

I know I shouldn't divide the best parts of me.

Can't remember the last time I was able to

give you my undivided attention;

Without thinking of the options I weigh.

Entertaining my selfish ways…

The best option is to choose me.

So I chose to hold onto my faith,

hold onto my heart,

hold onto my peace,

hold on to the little bit I got left,

hold on for dear life.

Nobody warns you about times like this

where you have to do it scared and alone.

Where you have to really follow your heart

because that's the only place you can call home.

Because what are you settling for?

What's the sacrifice?

How much is all this going to cost you?

Could it be your whole life?

What are you fighting for?

What if I said let's not fight anymore.

Lets surrender to the way of the divine

because we both know you have options too

And I'll never tell you to pick me

Pick me

Pick me

Pick me

She's already been chosen.

The choices we make define our life.

Choose wisely.

Born to Die

As my cat lays next to me purring loudly,

I know how happy she is to call this home.

But the voice inside my head says

''She won't live very long.

You'll have to bury her soon.''

Then I get a call from my father

He asks me if I prayed today.

He told me he can't move his left hand

but he keeps his right on the bible.

He told me he feels closer to God.

He told me the stitches on his chest have finally healed

but it breaks my heart every time

knowing he ain't got much left.

When my mother leaves for work

I see how she gathers her aching bones.

When she comes home,

I hear the way she sighs.

I can't deny her silent cries.

I never really seen her live,

I only seen her survive.

The truth is,

I'm watching everyone I love go.

I know how this ends.

Love is a losing game.

We're all born to die.

We all go at our own time;

but there's something comforting about the word *'we'*

A reminder that we are not alone in our pain.

We are not alone in our grief.

we gather here.

October 31st

I have a ghost story to tell

about why the fall is orange

and why the wind leaves.

Perhaps, there is life unseen.

Today you celebrate, today I grieve.

Orange cat, why must you leave?

Today you trick or treat;

dressed in black and blood.

You really match the season.

For me, today has a different meaning.

I like to believe God wears me like a costume

and I have angels surrounding me;

Protecting me from evil spirits.

So while you're out chasing the wind;

being everyone but yourself,

I'll stay protected. Protecting my peace.

Letting the orange rest into the night

because *orange is the new black.*

November

November, I trust you to fall into place.
To show your bare limbs we call branches
and remind us all of your bittersweetness.
It is your gray that is gloomy
and I can't tell if the silence comforts me
or haunts every bone in my body.
I am anchored to the truth you never fail to reveal.
Yet, still I rise.
In the middle of my life transitioning
into the next phase of existence.
November, I trust you to fall into place.
I trust that what's coming is greater than
what has come and gone.
I smile with tears in my eyes
because nobody talks about how
grief and joy can sit in the same room.
Or about how closing the door on your old life
and locking in with your new life can be a lot to grasp.
But every November we're reminded.

Losing Control

It's been a while since we've spoken.

How come it always goes like that?

No, we can't pick up where we left off.

I'm too evolved.

I'm too far gone.

I'm officially over it.

I know you're reading this and it's too late.

Save your apologies.

Save the flowers you sent to me.

Save your tears.

No need to cry over spilt milk.

You cheated on yourself.

I can't come kiss it better.

You had me questioning where I went wrong.

So say goodbye to the good times.

So close yet so distant.

We were almost there but almost is never enough.

You missed me, I missed you too.

I guess we were just passing through a moment in time.

You were never meant to truly be mine.

We should've listened to the signs.

I should've left you at the first red flag

but we started playing tag.

It turned toxic.

How do we stop it?

Letting go of the hold;

Losing control…

Ready or Not

At the end of the day,

when every moment has passed

and lives only in our memory;

I remember your laugh.

I remember the way you used to look at me.

I remember your smell.

I also remember the last thing you said to me…

"I'll see you later"

Later came and I'll never be able to see you again.

Perhaps, you meant I'll see you in everything else.

Your ghost haunts me and I can't get your voice out of my head.

I see your shadow in all your favorite places.

I go and sit in your spot hoping the moment will hold me

just a little while longer.

We never got to say goodbye.

I realized that we never will.

We never will receive closure.

Because life doesn't wait for nobody to be ready.

Grief is the place we go when we loved deeply in life.

Rest

Today I decided I'll get some rest.

I'll rise when my body feels like it.

I've worked long hours.

My body aches.

I deserve a break.

Before I break.

I showed up as much as I could.

Some days life requires us to slow down.

Rest days are productive too.

2034

Grand rising,

I woke up in the 9 year… again.

Last time we saw a time like this it was 2016…2025…

History repeats itself and has a funny way of saying

'see you next time'

With every breath, with every choice;

We shape the world and find our voice.

Mars rules and it's the season for action and transformation.

This is the end of the beginning.

The beginning of the end.

Another cycle.

Another shift.

Another change.

When the world opens its portal to jump timelines.

The chaos has a lot of folks crashing out.

I hope you see it through and through.

I've seen people lose

their life from the lack of self enlightenment.

Which is a disease within itself.

Bring your shadows to face the light.

Let the sun kiss you and say goodbye to the fight.

In endings, we see how far we've grown.

From deep down where a seed was sown.

The world is inviting us to stand and grow tall.

Through lessons learned and battles won.

We move as one beneath the sun.

A year of courage, a year of grace.

To step into change, to find our place.

They thought I'd surrender to their program but I remembered my soul contract.

God is Love

War,

violence,

earth shaking,

global warming,

the rise of the seven seas,

and the fall of the great,

the wild west, who isn't as united as proclaimed to be,

when we're going against our own kind.

The devil thrives on division.

But I'm here to remind you that at some point,

we will birth a new world and a new life

in the midst of chaos and destruction.

The key

is

God

is

Love.

Lost In Translation

We have to study the history of science

to understand how we made it here.

History is not only the evolution of technology,

It's the evolution of provoking thoughts.

The modern age is human mastery over the material world.

It's returning to spirit and remembering

what we've forgotten in the process.

We are entering a new golden era of consciousness.

This is when humanity remembers its sacred connection to

earth, each other and source.

We know that nothing and nobody can play God

because nothing and no one is above God.

No matter what brilliant creations have been brought to life.

They will fight against this because
it challenges their religious beliefs.
It takes a lot of courage to rise above and seek more than
what you've been taught or influenced to believe.
This is not news, this is ancient wisdom.
For centuries we have been at war.
The battle has always been spiritual.

For ages we lost ourselves to the development of economics,
instead of the development of culture.
Culture is the heartbeat of humanity.
It connects people to each other,
to the past and to their purpose.

Divine Timing

One day I hope you will see why God made you wait.
Why you should take your time.
Why you should be more patient.
May impatience not cause you to
run to crumbs before your feast arrives.
I know when it's my time I'll be ready.
I had to take time to prepare.
Couple things I have to do before I get to meet you.
A couple things I never knew would teach me how to treat you.

The sequence of my life seems out of order
But I see why it had to happen like that as I get older.
The line up is crazy.
You gotta trust the process.
You gotta surrender to the flow.
Slow and steady wins the race.
I know consistency is key, that's why I go at my own pace.
I never questioned the timing of which things happened.
I know everything happens divinely.

One day I hope you see why God made you let go.
Why you should let go of your control.
Why you should let go of your perception of a good thing;
Maybe it's not good for you.
Maybe you should let it go… for good.
Maybe it didn't happen like that
because it was supposed to happen like this.
You know rejection is God's protection.
What if that redirection leads you to your glory.

Glory is a present.
A present you get when you stop focusing on what isn't.

I learned that you won't age well if
you don't know how to cope with nostalgia.
Careful not to stay too long visiting those memories;
You don't live there anymore.
What if I told you something better is on the way
but you're too busy blocking your blessings.

One day I hope you learn your lesson.
One day I hope you see why God has a better plan for you.
But you can only see it through when you trust his guidance.
Tune into your divine and you will arrive right on time.

The Promise Land

I've come to the epiphany that there is no death.

Only shedding a part of this journey

to spiritually ascend higher and higher.

Spirit is a traveler.

Traveling to places only awakened souls can meet you;

For they have done the work for themselves.

They know what it looks like.

It looks like a light body amongst light bodies.

Can you recognize spirit?

Can you read energy?

That's what comes with the territory.

The only way to win is when you get right within,

says a Hill named Lauryn.

The mission is yours.

Nobody tells you that the light at the end of the tunnel is you all along.

The best version of yourself *is* the promise land.

I hope you made it home safe.

Glory

Are you able to recognize when

you're living in answered prayers?

Have you taken a moment of silence to thank God?

Not only for where you are but for where he brought you from?

Only God knows what it takes to

make it through the chapters of your life.

It's a blessing to be here.

The glory is all God.

When I look back to see how far I've come,

I only see one set of footsteps and they are not mine.

Although, a footprint may all look the same,

I know it was him who carried me.

Golden Key

24 karats sit on my collarbone

as I sit at the edge of the world all alone.

Wondering who will find me here?

Who travels to the end of the rainbow?

Who searches for the pot of gold?

Who has a key to hold?

Do they know the treasure is here?

Right in my chest, a heart of gold.

Through mountains, through valleys,

way over the hills.

May the road rise up to meet you;

To meet me here.

Who will find little ol' me?

Who holds the golden key?

Lucky you or lucky me?

Champagne & Ecstasy

Ecstasy is more about the energy

than it's ever been about pill popping.

I just had to clear the air.

The energy is high vibrational.

Ask me how I'm feeling and I'll tell you sensational.

A lot to be proud of now.

The blues can't keep me down.

I can care less about the talk of the town.

What goes around comes around

and a lot of ya'll got bad karma hunting you down.

I can't champagne toast with folks who

spill the tea when I'm not around

or kicked me when I was down.

The dirt they threw on my name fertilized me to grow.

I'm finding a new part of me to explore.

It's like I'm aging backwards;

Imagine me at 34.

I'm learning how to be greater than I was before.

Life will really have you checking yourself at the door

or checking yourself on the way out.

Everyone invited to the party is grown and mature.

Members only because I can't hang with

people who make me feel unsure.

Only champagne toasting with those who

understand what we came for.

Cheers!

Be For Real

I don't want to sell my stories anymore.

I want them to be forgotten.

I want them to be remembered in real life.

My life is my poetry.

Poetry is my love.

My love is not up for sale.

You can't buy your way here.

You can't touch this kind of intimacy.

You can't touch this kind of safety.

You only know this world;

you're such an earth child.

I'm talking about something otherworldly.

But you've never stepped outside for real

and it's not your fault.

Some things can't be told

you just had to be there…

I don't want to sell my stories anymore.

I want them to be forgotten.

I want them to be remembered in real life.

To be known is to be loved.

9 Lives

I've lived many lives.

I've seen many eyes.

Many suns, plenty of times.

Like the stars in a dark blue sky;

I dance on the edge of a new life.

I lost track of time but I know I was born

on the 9th day of saving the light.

I love every life but now

I get to live my best one yet.

Saturn Return

The sky whispers ''It is time to own your life.

Rise, my love, it's your turn.''

Rising the sun to shine light on every shadow.

Shaking my snowglobe until finally – I'm awake!

It feels like summer in December

Teaching me that endings are birthplaces.

Teaching me that bending without breaking

Means I learned to flex my abilities.

Resilience at its finest.

I've built character and strength

through discipline and dedication.

This is patience on paper.

For all the times I've lost my mind

trying to return

back to

self.

Come As You Are

The duality of life crashes…

The way rhythm has blues,
like rock always rolls,
like bow meets arrow,
the way Romeo kisses Juliet,
like lock needs key.

Do you find yourself getting lost
in this everchanging reality?
All you really have to be is here.
Here is a present for you.

Laugh now, cry later.
Everything good is over before you know it.
Please don't miss this moment.
Let's just hold it for as long as life grants.

The duality of life crashes once again;

For one cannot exist without the other.

Like ignorance is bliss but knowledge is power.

You can have fear but let bravery speak louder.

Everything is black and white.

But get under anyone's skin,

we can all paint the town red.

The world is binary but spirit is not.

You don't need to wait for the perfect time

or until you have this or that.

All of it is an illusion to postpone your success.

Come as you are.

It all exists here.

Apple Tree

In the orchard of my days,

I have learned that life

Is both seed and season.

The apple doesn't fall far from the tree

and I see it in the children I teach.

Their voices carry echoes of those before them.

Their dreams are historic.

I love watering wonder.

Guiding each bud to bloom.

But I don't get to decide the fate of fruit.

But what is nourished here,

will someday feed the world.

Surrender

It all started at rock bottom.

So deep in my blues;

I had to keep swimming.

To find the light,

to find myself,

to find my purpose.

I had to get closer to God.

I had to understand my assignment.

I had to carry that vision out.

I had to lead by example

and the only thing you should follow is your north star.

On the rise,

sometimes life will take us to great heights

just so we can remember how important the ground is.

The foundation is everything.

It teaches us how to swim.

Despite the pressure, despite the odds.

You can't get too caught up in illusion.

Take the rose colored glasses off.

See it for what it really is.

The journey is a marathon.

With ascension comes turbulence.

I knew it would be a rocky road

but I'm learning to enjoy the ride.

Even with detours and redirection,

I'm trusting God's plan.

Even when we don't have the whole thing mapped out,

try to remember that you are not lost,

this is what exploring looks like.

Sometimes the awakening is rude

and it forces us out of our comfort zone

but the growth is honorable.

Eventually, we become so elevated

that we are no longer connected to our past.

That's how you know you're passed that level

and it's on to the next…

Grand rising,

I've risen like a phoenix from the ashes.

It took everything in me to get up today.

The sun isn't always out to play.

The rain makes me feel some kind of way.

I've been trying to find a way to let this feeling go…

I'll go shower now

before the rest of the world awakens.

I let the water wash away my sins

trying to remind myself…

The rising is grand even when I feel small.

Don't think this is a smooth sailing ride.
Sometimes we get caught in the riptides but
we learn how to surf.

How can we show up as our best selves
if we haven't seen our worst?

After experiencing death a few times,
the only way I made it out alive...

I surrendered to the divine.

The End & The Beginning

What happens after?

You wake up…again.

Death is not the end.

It's the beginning of the next chapter.

Changing the scenery

You spend another lifetime remembering

what's already been written.

You exit the stage to meet the author.

May the sun kiss you into awakening.

May the moon light your shadows.

May the wind carry whispers of love.

May the rain cleanse all that no longer serves you.

May your courage outshine your fear.

May you trust the unfolding of time.

May grace become your best friend.

May you forever flirt with your own truth.

May you pray it all into alignment.

May you always find your way home.

May the key to it all be within you.

www.ingramcontent.com/pod-product-compliance
Lightning Source LLC
Chambersburg PA
CBHW031811220426
43662CB00007B/602